MW00979347

intro**duction**

This booklet is divided into seven areas of discussion. Each week you will explore a different topic.

The course will be most effective when used in a small group setting of three to ten people with an obvious leader to facilitate discussion.

It is very important to complete the entire course or you may be left with an imbalanced perspective.

This course is designed in a manner that you can explore Christianity as a group - your opinion is always valued. Do not be afraid to speak your mind.

Be careful not to dominate the discussion but let others have adequate time to respond and offer their input. Hopefully the course will be a time where you receive encouragement and feel free to express your feelings as well as your thoughts.

The reflect pages are a place for you to reflect, journal or take notes. The Bible verses on these pages develop the themes of each section a little further.

The Bible, essentially, is a collection of 66 smaller books, all under one cover. To find a specific Bible reference in Exploring Christianity, go to the book listed (i.e. John). The numbers (for example, 3.16) refer to the chapter and verse of the book.

tableof**contents**

written and developed by mark dowds
design and photography by joshua dunford and joy dutcher
edited by jordan bateman

copyright © 2001 fresh initiatives, inc. manufactured and distributed under license by fresh**resource**
check our website, http://www.fresh**resource**.com, for notes, information, and help

Scripture quotations marked (NIV) are taken from the HOLY BIBLE, NEW INTERNATIONAL VERSION.
NIV. Copyright 1973, 1978, 1984 by International Bible Society. Used by permission of Zondervan
Publishing House. All rights reserved.

topicone {life}

>If you were stranded on a desert island and received two wishes, what would they be? (You cannot wish to leave the island)

"Life is like a box of chocolates, you never know what you're going to get."

- Forrest Gump

>What do you think of Forrest Gump's philosophy of life?
>What is your theory on life?

"The universe and human existence are without a purpose and therefore devoid of meaning."

- Kurt E.M. Baier (a leading humanist)

>Do you think there is a significant purpose or meaning to our existence?
>What do you think most people look for in life?
>What do you think is the answer or the missing piece?

There are many who would strongly disagree with Kurt Baier's ideas and statements. They instinctively know or want to believe that we are here for a reason, that our lives have some form of significance. Few of us want to accept an idea that we are just an accident or a mistake. We have a built in desire to know our worth.

Pascal observed that most people were searching for something they couldn't explain. He noticed that they were willing to try almost anything in the hope that it would bring the fulfilment they were looking for. Most wasted their lives chasing after the wind. He offered a valid suggestion: "There is a God-shaped vacuum in every heart."

Read **John 6.1-13** - Feeding the 5,000

Thousands of people followed Jesus because they saw Him heal the sick and do a lot of miraculous things. Not all of them believed in Him. Many didn't know who He really was but His actions created a lot of interest so many tagged along to investigate some more.

>What do you think about this story?
>Why would Jesus be interested in taking responsibility to feed all these people?
>Do you think there is a reason behind Jesus getting his disciples to start giving out the food?

reflect {topic**one**}

Jesus wants to see every person who is hungry fed. He doesn't want people who are hungry to be left without food. Modern day followers of Jesus can be found helping those who are poor and in need. Jesus said that the kingdom of God was good news to the poor.

Jesus said:"*I am the bread of life. He who comes to me will never go hungry, and he who believes in me will never be thirsty.*"

- John 6.35

Have you ever felt like there is a missing piece in your life? An empty space inside? What does it feel like? What other things do we often use to try and fill the gap? Do you think that Jesus could miraculously fill your emptiness/hunger?

warning:sharp

(use this space to journal your thoughts)
Colossians 1.16; John 10.10; Jeremiah 29.11

getting**personal**

Judith Bell
(Northern Ireland)

I am 17 years old and I live in Bangor, Northern Ireland. I grew up in a Christian home and I always went to church and was expected to do all the 'churchie' stuff. I think I really decided to make a commitment to God when I was about 13. God really touched my life. I used just to go to church and hate it. But when God touched me, I began to really get excited about going to church and experiencing Him. He spoke to me and challenged me about stuff I was doing in my life, like swearing and doing all the stuff that teenagers do. I tried to ignore Him but realized that I really couldn't go on like that forever and needed to sort myself out.

Since then, I can definitely say that I have experienced God big time working in my life. He has helped me to get over things that I found really difficult and deal with stuff, which I had hidden away, hoping I would never remember. God has spoken to me so much and has really blessed me. I now am doing things in church that I never in a million years thought I would do! God has used me. And although I still find stuff hard, I know that God will never leave me and no matter how many times I mess up, He's going to forgive me every time.

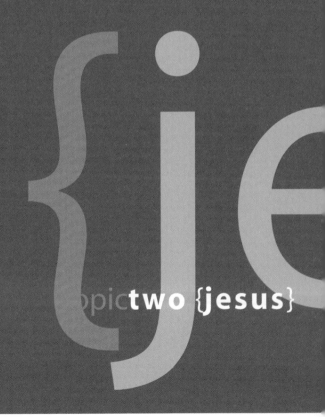

topic**two** {jesus}

>What was your favorite piece of clothing while you were at primary school?

By the time Jesus was in his thirties, there were many differing opinions to who He was. This is why Jesus turned to his friends and asked, *'**Who do the people say I am?**'* They responded by saying: *'**Some say John the Baptist; others say Elijah; and still others, one of the prophets.**'* **(Mark 8.27-28)**

>If Jesus asked the same question in this century, what do you think would be the list of answers He would get?

After Jesus had heard the list of answers His friends had given, He went one step further and asked, "But what about you, who do you say I am?" Peter answered, "You are the Christ."

>What would your answer be and why?
>Why do you think Jesus asked these questions in the first place?

One thing is for sure: Jesus wasn't trying to find out who He was. He appeared to be very confident about knowing who He was and what He was about. Jesus, on many occasions, revealed who He was by what many now call his I am statements.

I am the Light of the World. I am the Way, the Truth, and the Life. I am the Resurrection and the Life. I am the Gate. I am the True Vine. I am the Bread of Life. I am the Good Shepherd.

Take some time to discuss what Jesus was claiming when He said these things.

Read **Mark 14.53-65** - Jesus being judged by the religious leaders

>Do you think that Jesus would have faced persecution and death if He had been fabricating who He was?

The title Christ is the same as Messiah or Anointed One. It was a Kingly title that was used for the One many where waiting for to save the world.

SUS

THRIFT
STORE

OPEN

reflect {topictwo}

Make a top three 'I am' list of your own that describes who you are and what you're about. Use one to describe your relationship to Jesus (e.g., friend/stranger/afraid etc.).

> _____

> _____

> _____

>Are you content with who you are?
>Are you content with how you presently relate to Jesus?

warning:**sharp**

(**use this space to journal your thoughts**)
Philippians 2.1-11; John 12.12-19;
John 7.25-43; John 7.1-30.

gettingpersonal

Tobey Mackinnon
(British Columbia, Canada)

I grew up in a very strict and legalistic atmosphere. I went to private school, had a strict home, and a strict church. I had never understood God. All He was to me was a big scary higher power that hated me if I was bad. When I was 13, things in my life started going downhill. My parents fought a lot; I got into trouble all the time. By the time I was 14, I was anorexic, doing pot, drinking and partying. It progressed through grades 8 and 9, getting more serious. I began to experiment with satanic worship and thought about suicide more. I would slash my wrists, drink alcohol or take drugs so that I would feel better. Deep down there was always an empty space.

Life was pretty bad when I got expelled from school in grade 9. Then I met some people who seemed different to me. There was something about them that I liked. They invited me to go with them on a road trip. I was reluctant to go but I was intrigued to find out what it was that made them different. By the second night of the camp I had observed enough to know that I wanted what they had: Jesus. As soon as I let Jesus into my life the cravings for cigarettes, LSD, and guys left me. I wanted more of Jesus instead. The scars on my wrists were completely healed as well as the years of emotional pain. God is my hope now. He is all I need to get high. I am a completely different person today. God has filled the emptiness and He keeps blessing me and healing me. Life is still not easy but I have peace now. I know that God loves me and that I am valuable with a purpose on earth.

topicthree {god the father

>What was your favorite childhood toy? Why?

Childhood can be a very different experience for every person. Some things we enjoy talking about, other things we'd rather forget. Although some of us may not know our biological dads, we can recognize similarities between parents and children.

>When someone mentions the word 'Father,' what images and words spring to mind?

Read **Luke 15.11-32** - The Prodigal Son

>What is your opinion of the father in this story?
>What impressive characteristics does he have in the story?
>How does the father in this story compare with your own father?

The Bible refers to God as Father on many occasions. It also refers to those who believe in Him as being His children. The Father in the story is a picture of who God is and how He treats His family.

>When someone has recited the Lord's prayer - 'Our Father in Heaven ...',
 is this the sort of father you have pictured in your mind?
>How does this affect your view of God?
>Who would you compare yourself with in the story and why?

What are some of the more noticeable similarities you have observed among parents and children that you know?

>The Bible tells us that we have all been made in the image of God. What part of God's image do you think is still obvious in you?

Many people think that to become a Christian they have to look good and be capable of doing the right things. This is a common misconception. When someone becomes a Christian, they join the family of God and immediately their Father in heaven begins a process that changes them from the inside out. Over the entirety of their lives, from that point on, they begin to grow to be more like Him. They begin to look like Jesus, the perfect Son of God. God does the work in us; He only calls us to be willing to change. This process also leads us to be free from other's expectations and free to be who we were created to be. It is a miraculous work of God.

>Have you ever seen someone you know be changed for the better after becoming a Christian?

ner}

reflect topic**three}**

List three characteristics of the Father you would like Him to form in you.

> _____

> _____

> _____

warning slippery when wet

(use this space to journal your thoughts)
Matthew 6.5-14; John 8.42-47; John 10.22-42

gettingpersonal

Sam Halliday
(Northern Ireland)

Up until January 1998, my life had consisted of alcohol and the occult, and I had started to become a womanizer. It was actually a dodgy time for me, because although I only practiced white magic (or the supposedly good kind), I had intended to take up black magic (the definitely BAD kind), because I wasn't getting what I wanted.

Then, through coincidence, I fancied a girl who went to a local church. In an attempt to win her, I decided to go along. A couple of my other Christian friends also attended. I went on the Sunday night and I witnessed people actually being passionate about God in a way I had never known before. Something I can't even describe now just told me this was right, and over the next few months I kind of drifted into Christianity. Somewhere along the way since then I have dedicated my entire life to God, and I have forgotten about the girl (who, incidentally, I did win… for a while).

topic**four** {faith}

>Tell the story of the worst hairstyle you ever had. Be honest.

Video Clip: Indiana Jones and the Last Crusade - the leap of faith
Watch the video from when Indiana's dad gets shot through to walking over the invisible bridge.

The Bible tells us to *'live by faith, not by sight'*.

- 2 Corinthians 5.7

Read **Hebrews 11.7-11**

>How do think Noah and Abraham became confident to do something that seemed weird?
>Why could Indiana Jones trust the words of an old tattered book?

Faith is being sure of what we hope for and certain of what we do not see.

- Hebrews 11.1

Many people fear stepping out and putting their faith in God because they think life will end for them. They think that becoming a Christian means that life revolves around drinking tea and having Bible studies with old people. This is a wrong perception. The experience of the fullness of life only begins when someone puts their faith in God. Jesus said, "I have come that they may have life, and have it to the full." If you take some time to read about Jesus, He did not live a boring or uneventful life. He was the picture of life itself.

Faith comes from hearing the message, and the message is heard through the word of Christ.

- Romans 10.17

The Bible is like a manual for life. God made us and gave us an instruction manual to teach us how we can function best. All of the Bible is inspired by God. Read it with a listening ear and God will direct you. **2 Timothy 3.16-17** says, "*All Scripture is God-breathed and is useful for teaching, rebuking, correcting, and training in righteousness, so that the child of God may be thoroughly equipped for every good work.*" The more we follow God's instructions and find that they work, the more we have faith to go further.

>Have you ever read the Bible or tried to use it as a manual for life?

ith

reflect {topic**four**}

List three issues in your life you would like God to speak to you about.

> _____

> _____

> _____

warning:**falling rocks**

(**use this space to journal your thoughts**)
Romans 10.17; Hebrews 11; Matthew 17.20;
James 2.18; 2 Corinthians 5.7

gettingpersonal

Jeremy Crowle
(British Columbia, Canada)

My family has been church-oriented since I was born. We've always had a pretty structured relationship with each other, which meant it was hard to communicate about what we knew about Jesus personally.

My father started a church when I was seven years old. We all pitched in, and began to build what was to become one of the smallest churches in history. Don't get me wrong, it was a great church. Five years later, we began to join hands with a bigger church, and it eventually started to grow. One day, my dad found out the church (that had joined with us) had been taking a large sum of the money from us to make their church bigger. It was a really hard time for us, because we had put a lot of our lives into it. My family left that church and we didn't attend a church for years after. I went to high school and did my own thing. I made friends that also lived their own lives and we all had a great unfulfilling time. One of my friends overdosed and died, another friend did so many drugs that he lost his ability to speak and walk. I had moved out and was traveling across the country in search of happiness but I couldn't find anything. I became depressed and desperate. My girlfriend had been going to church back home, and I had been thinking a lot about going to church with her. She was meeting a lot of cool people there, not like the "Christians" I had known in the past. One guy (who is now one of my best friends) began to tell me who Jesus really was and what He could do for me. It was the best thing to think of a God that wanted to hang out with me, as much I needed Him. My girlfriend and I started going to church. The people were a lot more passionate there. It was inspiring. I began planning my life. I went to art school, started to paint, got a job, and was doing a lot better. But it didn't end there. I discovered that it wasn't just being happy that being a Christian was about. Another friend of mine told me about making disciples. It was strange talking to my old friends about Jesus. They didn't know what to do, but they were as desperate as I was, but as soon as they saw how much I had changed, they were sold on Jesus too.

My father still doesn't go to church, but he knows what God is doing in me. It's the most important thing that ever happened in my life. Because someone believed in me, I know how to believe in my friends. And I know that Jesus will believe in them, also.

topic**five** {forgiveness}

>If you could be a cartoon character, who would you be? Why?

Briefly analyze your life and try to place yourself on the grid line with an 'x'.

Bad   Good

_____

1   2   3   4   5   6   7   8   9   10

>Explain why you have put yourself at this number on the grid.
>What would someone have to do to be marked around '1'?
>Do you think it is possible for anyone to be marked around '10'?
>What do you think of when someone mentions 'sin'?

The Bible tells us that the wages of sin is death and that without being saved from our situation we will remain separated from God and everything He desires to share with us.

>How does this discussion make you feel?

Read **John 12.46-47** and **1 Timothy 1.15**

>Is this good news to you?

Sin is like breaking the law. There are consequences and penalties every time we break it. If we are caught breaking the speed limit, we will get a fine that we have to pay by a certain date or there will be further consequences. Because we are sinful people we have a drawer full of unpaid tickets. We are incapable of repaying God. We need help. This is why Jesus died on the cross 2,000 years ago. God knew we were in a hopeless situation but because He loved us so much He sent his only Son to take our place and die to pay for our sins so that we could be free again. This is how Jesus saves us. All someone has to do is accept what has been done for them to receive the freedom from the fear of death and the hope of a new life that starts now.

The word 'sin' is an old English word used in archery. When an archer misses the target the score keeper shouts 'Sin'. Sin, in its true form, means to miss the target. **Romans 3.23** tells us that we have all missed God's target. None of us have a clear 10. We have all sinned, some more, some less.

reflect {topicfive⟩

>Do you understand why Jesus died on a cross for you?

John 3.16 and 17 says: "For God so loved the world that He gave his one and only Son, that whoever believes in Him shall not perish but have eternal life. For God did not send His Son into the world to condemn the world but to save the world through Him."

>What do you think is an appropriate response to what Jesus has done for us?

>Does this make sense to you?

{lick} and**stick**

– ✂ –

(**use this space to journal your thoughts**)
John 8.1-11; Romans 10.9; John 1.12;
John 10.10; Colossians 1.14

gettingpersonal
Joey Courchesne
(Canada)

I didn't come from a Christian home, but my parents did raise me in a very strict one. So I guess I've always grown up with some sort of morals. I knew that there was something else 'out there' bigger than us but never thought much about God. I filled this hole as a teenager with drugs, alcohol, partying and even exploring some new age philosophy. A couple of years ago, I accepted the new age philosophy but didn't get involved in it or practice it. Around that time, I had a couple of friends who were Christians and I would always argue with them about God. I argued that He did not exist and that Christianity was something to believe in for weak people. I told them that it was outdated, and it did not apply today. So I asked one of them if I could prove to her that Christianity was a hoax. I told her that I would go to her church and expose its holes. I won't forget the day I stepped into that church. Even though I knew all the kids there as the geeks from high school, something was there that I had never known before. I was drawn back there, Sunday after Sunday, and to the youth group events as well. A couple of months later I repented and Jesus forgave me. My friends all thought I was crazy. They knew me as the one who was the most anti-Christian.

I was delivered almost immediately out of drugs, alcohol and partying. The old new age beliefs were replaced with the truth. Now God is doing amazing work in my life. He is blessing my time at home with my family and restoring my lost relationships with them and ministering to them through me. He has burdened us to ask him daily for the salvation of our city. That has led to the formation of small cell groups devoted to that cause. Also, God has set up interdenominational worship gatherings both inside and outside the church. I have seen God work to change the lives of people we have prayed for. He is so faithful in breaking down walls and sending His Holy Spirit to us. The blessings continue.

topic**six** {the holy spirit}

>Share the most memorable two weeks of your life in two minutes.

>When someone says 'Holy Spirit,' what springs to your mind?
>What stories have you heard about the Holy Spirit?
>What concerns do you have about this part of Christianity?

Read **John 3.5-8**

>Why do you think the Holy Spirit is so important if we are to be reborn and have a new start in life?

The Holy Spirit is the person who comes to live in us when we become a Christian. He is the person who speaks to us and helps us to change. **Romans 8.15** refers to the Holy Spirit as the Spirit of sonship. He is the One who transforms us into the image of Jesus. He leads us to live like Jesus. **Galatians 5.22** tells us that the fruit of the Holy Spirit is love, joy, peace, patience, kindness, goodness, faithfulness, gentleness, and self-control. This is what grows in us as we mature as a Christian.

Read **Acts 2.1-13**
>What happens to people when they are filled with the Holy Spirit?
>Why do you think they were accused of having too much wine?

Read **Acts 2.14-22** and **38-41**
>Who can be filled with the Holy Spirit?
>How can someone be filled with the Holy Spirit?

The Holy Spirit is one person of the Trinity. He thinks, speaks, leads and can be offended as any person can. He is sometimes referred to as the Spirit of Jesus. He is God Himself at work. An encounter of the Holy Spirit is always a personal, rather than an impersonal, experience. Because it is so personal to who we are as individuals, we react in different manners when the Holy Spirit comes upon us. What happens in the physical is just a sign that something deep is happening within us.

If you would like to become a Christian, please say so to the leader of the group and they will pray with you and for the Holy Spirit to come and fill you. If you are already a Christian and would like to be filled with the Holy Spirit, ask the leader of the group to pray for you.

irit}

reflect {topicsix}

The fruit of the Holy Spirit is love, joy, peace, patience, kindness, goodness, faithfulness, gentleness, and self-control. Which three of these fruit have you obviously grown in over the past year?

> _____

> _____

> _____

caution:**hot** ✂

(**use this space to journal your thoughts**)
Luke 11.9-13; John 15.26; 2 Corinthians 13.14;
Matthew 28.19; 2 Corinthians 3.17; Acts 9.1-7

gettingpersonal

Lisa Walraven
(British Columbia , Canada)

Ever since I can remember, I have had some sort of a concept of God. I recall walking down my street at ten years old to go to church one Sunday morning. I had no real reason to go other than the fact that I had a nice cross necklace to wear and for some reason I wanted to go to church. So I did. I don't remember much from that morning, but two things stuck out: Jesus is always with us and He loves us.

Four years later a friend of mine invited me to go to youth group with her and some of our friends. For us, the "non-Christians," youth group was hanging out in the parking lot of a church and harassing the Christians inside by throwing various objects at the windows and chasing each other around the neighborhood. This church is, and has been, the drug-trading center of the neighborhood and as a result, many of my seemingly innocent friends started to experiment with drugs. I will never forget the night I first saw my best friend trying to hide a joint from me. Trying to impress her "friends," she smiled at me as if it were no big deal while she shamefully held the joint behind her back. I didn't know what to say or do so I turned away and walked across the parking lot. I started shaking and felt like I was going to start crying (which was totally unusual for me as I was not really an emotional person... well, not in public anyhow). I sat down underneath a tree and looked out at the parking lot. In one corner, my friends were smoking up. In another, two guys, surrounded by cheering onlookers, beat each other up. People were running and screaming all over the place. It was spiritual and physical chaos. Suddenly I saw how fake and meaningless my life was. What was I doing? I started to cry. A friend of mine sat down beside me. He asked me what was wrong, and just as he asked, my eyes lifted toward the church. Through an open door I saw a group of people of all ages singing and talking with Jesus. The room seemed to glow; it seemed so warm. My friend asked me again, "Lisa, what's wrong?" I replied to him between sobs, "I don't know, but next time, I'm going inside." So I did. I met Jesus shortly after and immediately knew that I had found the way, the truth and the real life. Today, He is my source, my life and my guide. The best part about that group of people I used to hang out with is that over half of them are saved now, too. I didn't reject them because of what they were doing, but because I loved them as Jesus loved me they got to know Jesus, too.

topic**seven** {church life}

>Share one of your most embarrassing moments.

The Christian church is a relic of a bygone era; a monument to religious sentiment in the past.

>How would you respond to the above statement?
>Have you ever had an experience of church? What was it like?
>Is it possible that church could become relevant to you and your culture?

The Greek word for church is ekklesia, which simply means a gathering of people. The church is the people. Everything else, including the building, is an instrument to facilitate Christian community.

Read **Acts 2.38-47.** Make a list of characteristics that describe the early church.
>What grabs your attention about this story?
>What parts of the story are you not sure about?

>If church was a bunch of real, transparent and loving people, would it be something you would consider being part of?

One of the most exciting parts of being part of a local church is participating as a member of a small group. A small group is a place to encounter Jesus, a place to belong, a place to grow, a place to give, and a place to reach out. A church small group is very similar to what you have just experienced by going through this short course. It can be with your friends and can be led by a friend. Would you like to be part of a small group or would you like us to develop this group into a church small group that can meet anywhere?

How can the leader of this course help you from this point onwards, other than being a good friend?

>Did you enjoy this course? What would you change about it?
>What has been the highlight of this course for you?

ife}

reflect {topicseven⟩

topicseven {church life}_ 46

ife}

reflect {topicseven⟩

What three things have surprised you about Christianity?

> _____

> _____

> _____

warning:blunt

(use this space to journal your thoughts)
Acts 4.32-37; 5.12-16; Ephesians 2.1-10

gettingpersonal

Scott Cave
(British Columbia, Canada)

Jesus was a carpenter. I was an electrician. I suppose, in a way, Jesus is just like the guy down the street who gets up in the morning, eats his breakfast, brushes his teeth and takes off to work. Well, maybe He doesn't do that much anymore, He's probably got more pressing matters. Like preventing creation from tearing at the seams; or listening to every heart on earth, as if each one were His only child. But there was a day when He did, get up, wash Himself, kiss His mother good-bye and head off to work for the day.

It seems like a long time ago now, but I can remember when the thought of having The Almighty as a personal friend was incomprehensible. These days we're pretty tight. There are days that I forget to call Him up, but like any true friend, He's always happy to hear from me when I do. I'm sure He'd like to hear from me more often, but I can always be confident that He'll listen to me on the same personal level that He always does.

I can't say that there was a particular day that I met God. He just always seemed to be there. There was a day when my sister asked me if I would like to have God living inside my heart. It seemed pretty logical at the time. She led me through the prayer and minutes later, my heart contained eternity. I'm glad I was so young at the time, because I don't think I would be able to understand it as well if I had to do it all over again. Thankfully, eternity lasts forever.

There have been dark years in my life. Times when I explored the darkside, looking for the "force." I looked high and low. But was disappointed when I didn't find it in the acid, sex, or image-boosting social activities. All that led me to was depression, hopelessness, insecurity, and suicidal tendencies. I did find it though, in the most unlikely place. It was already inside of me, in a small pocket of eternity hidden within my heart. And it had a name, a face and a will, all its own. Its name was Jesus and He had been waiting for me. I was lying in bed one night. Living in Whistler, living it up. Living death. I thought back to a time when I felt safe and covered. Deep inside of me there was a voice. When it spoke, I was surprised to discover it was my own. "Jesus," it whispered, "I want that again. I want to feel like a child, safe in your arms. Innocent." After that day, the Force began to move me. Over a period of about two years, events led me back home, back into good relationships. Back to Jesus.
The story doesn't end there, but I can't tell you where it goes. It's somewhere in the future, beyond my vision. But He is there too, waiting for me, walking with me. He teaches me and laughs with me. He is my Brother, Captain, King, and Savior. But over and above He is my closest friend. We're on an adventure together and we're never turning back.

epi**logue** {commitment}

Becoming a Christian is about surrender. It is giving up on your own attempts to live right by handing the control of your life over to Jesus. It is about trusting Jesus to guide and direct you in every area of life. It is about preferring what God wants over what you want. It is about letting Jesus be Lord of your life.

Becoming a Christian is about becoming a friend of Jesus and enjoying a relationship with Him. It is not a religious exercise, it is accepting Jesus and learning to listen and talk with Him.

Becoming a Christian is about saying goodbye to your old lifestyle and being willing to follow Jesus.

Becoming a Christian is about saying sorry for your sin and accepting forgiveness.

Becoming a Christian is about saying thank you to Jesus for dying for you.

Becoming a Christian is about joining the family of God and getting connected with other believers in a church.

Romans 10.9-10 says: *"If you confess with your mouth, 'Jesus is Lord,' and believe in your heart that God raised Him from the dead, you will be saved. For it is with your heart that you believe and are justified, and it is with your mouth that you confess and are saved."*

If you would like to become a Christian, pray and ask Jesus to come into your life. You can do this anywhere. Use your own words or use the following prayer:

"Lord, I am sorry for how I have lived my life for myself, and I am sorry for sinning against You. Thank You for dying on the cross for me and for taking the punishment I deserve. I accept Your forgiveness and the life You want to give me. I am willing to change in any way You ask and I desire only to please You. So Lord, I ask You to come and live in me and make my life Your home. Holy Spirit, I ask You to come and empower me to live like Jesus. Change me and equip me to do all that You have planned for me."

After you have become a Christian, tell the leader of the group, your friends and family. Ask the leader and others to pray for you. Tell them how you feel and tell them where you need the most help, healing, and support.

reflect {epi**logue**}

(use this space to journal your thoughts)
James 5.16; Galatians 2.20;
Mark 16.15-20; Ephesians 5.18

gettingpersonal

Everyone has a testimony. After each section, you have gotten to look through a little window, into someone's life, and see how God has met them and how He has changed their lives. What has your journey through life been? How have you met God? What has He been saying to you? Don't try and compare your testimonies to other people's because we each need a unique statement about what God has done for us. God gives us different lives and experiences because through our different testimonies, we will each be able to help and love specific people.

As a group, share your testimonies with each other. It will be an amazing opportunity to learn about each other and how God has been impacting your lives.

other **resources available**

Experiencing Life

Experiencing Life was developed as a discussion tool for small groups. It is targeted towards those who have no church background or experience. It will work with youth in most small group settings within homes, schools, churches, missions, and camps. This booklet covers three main values that everyone encounters in life: loving, giving, and serving. The hope is that when someone is faced with a choice in life, after going through this course, they will have a reference to Jesus' life and the wisdom he has to offer.

Exploring Christianity

Exploring Christianity is an eight-week course designed to assist young people who are leading their friends to God. It teaches some of the foundational truths of Christianity while removing common roadblocks along the way. This course introduces people to a small group discussion setting that in turn will lead to an easy transition into further community based discipleship.

Reaching Out

Reaching Out is a tool that has been specifically written to help young people understand the principles of peer-led small groups. It is an effective resource and reference for young people who are actively leading their friends through the process of discipleship. Reaching Out gives clear guidelines to follow that allows the leader to be effective and flexible while developing people in a small group environment.

Following Jesus

Following Jesus is a training booklet that leads young people through several stages of growth in discipleship. This resource helps to break down the strategy and mission of Christ into a concise process in which to follow. It details how Jesus ministered with people and emphasizes the calling of all believers to continue with the commission to multiply the life and mission of Jesus in society.

W2 : Live Worship

W2 is a live album that captures the experience of two Canadian bands that share one passion to worship God. It has a fresh and edgy feel to what is happening within the present evolution of worship among youth. The uniqueness of this album is expressed in the depth of lyrical poetry and creative use of popular instruments.

>> available at **www.freshresource.com**

freshresource

+ ## MULTIPLYING THE LIFE AND
  ## MISSION OF JESUS AMONG YOUTH

+ our vision:
  To be an influential community and resource for missionaries in an emerging culture.

+ our mission:
  Multiplying the life and mission of Jesus among youth.

+ our challenge:
  Statistics show that the church is losing influence with this generation

+ our strategy:
  Making disciples, connecting people, and developing resources

www.freshresource.com

◯ flywheel 🇨🇦 TORONTO, CANADA

momentum FOR THE mission

Flywheel is a missionary training course that is equipping people to multiply the life and mission of Jesus in society. It is an eight-month residential missionary experience that engages the student with many of the "how-to's" of spiritual growth and leadership as well as the hands on experience of working with unchurched youth and church planting.

www.freshresource.com/flywheel